T0115074

STAND UP!

STAND UP!

For What You Believe In

Donna Jean Martin-Young

authorHOUSE®

AuthorHouse™
1663 Liberty Drive
Bloomington, IN 47403
www.authorhouse.com
Phone: 1-800-839-8640

Published by AuthorHouse   02/12/2013

ISBN: 978-1-4685-7431-9 (sc)
ISBN: 978-1-4685-7432-6 (e)

CONTENTS

CHAPTER 1   Breakfast With Ronald.........................1

CHAPTER 2   Ronald The School Bus Driver 5

CHAPTER 3   Career Day 7

CHAPTER 4   Good Deeds Get Wisdom 9

CHAPTER 5   The Big Decision.............................11

CHAPTER 6   Words of Wisdom............................15

CHAPTER 7   Sit-Ins..19

CHAPTER 8   The Sit-in Movement
                     My Brother's Part............................21

OVERVIEW 23

DEDICATION

*To my grandson Carmeron Reese, granddaughters
Raven and Makayla Martin, grandniece Aniyoh Martin,
grandnephew Avery Bruce Martin-Toe. To all children who
Stand Up! for what they believe is right
for their country, family and community.*

STAND UP!

"One aspect of the civil-rights struggle
that receives little attention is that the
contribution it makes to the whole society."

Martin Luther King Jr., 1963

CHAPTER 1
BREAKFAST WITH RONALD

I could tell it was 5 o'clock in the morning, when I heard our mom stirring around in the kitchen because that was the time she got up to cook breakfast. Mom seldom miss that time.

Next, there came the sweet smell of breakfast. We had eggs, sausage, grits, cheese toast and coffee. While mom was cooking, my two older brothers and I were sleeping in our beds. If the smell of the food did not wake us, surely the aroma from the coffee would wake us up. Mom and dad were talking very low, so we couldn't make out what they were talking about.

Since Ronald was the oldest child, he had to get up earlier then we did. Ronald struggled to get out from under the soft warm blue blanket that kept him warm each night. He would sit on the edge of the bed with his feet touching the cold floor gaining the courage to get up and head to the bathroom. It did not take very long for Ronald to brush his teeth, wash his face, and comb his hair. With the snap of his finger, Ronald's clothes were on his body and he was eager to wake up his younger sister and brother. He yelled, "Get up, Get up!" while touching their feet. "It is time to wash up and put your clothes on so we can eat our breakfast."

Our oldest brothers' command was taken seriously and was followed. Our family sat down to eat our breakfast. Dad had on his uniform and mom had on her all white uniform that was covered with her housecoat. Mom worked as a LPN (License Practical Nurse) at the old Columbia Hospital that was on Harden Street. My brothers and I wore our school clothes to the breakfast table too. I had on my beautiful yellow dress and my brothers wore their pants and a shirt. Ronald blessed our food with a short blessing. "Bless the food for the nourishmentof our body, Lord, and thank you mom for a good breakfast". After eating, mom begin cleaning the table and putting the dirty dishes in a pan of water while the rest of the family went in opposite directions. Dad drove his car to the post office, my brother and I walked two blocks to C.A. Johnson High School.

To Ronald, calculus and trigonometry was like "taking candy from a baby". Ronald told the story of when he was called to the board to solve a problem. His teacher called him Mr. Bus Driver. So the story went. "Mr. Bus Driver, come to the board," demanded the renowned math teacher, Mr. Taylor. Ronald's face would light up like a candle, glowing in the night. Ronald would pretend not to know how to do the problem on the way to the board, then, he would hesitantly find the answer. "Yes, that's it," said Mr. Taylor.

Mr. Taylor knew Ronald was playing around, but he did not know why. Ronald did not want to get picked on by other students if they knew he was gifted and made straight A's in math. One day Mr. Taylor asked Ronald, "Would you like to teach calculus for me on Career Day?" Ronald immediately replied, "Yes! Yes!" Ronald began to have second thoughts about the, Career Day thing. "Oh, boy, me as a calculus teacher, how am I going to explain that to my friends? What would my day be like teaching math?" thought Ronald to himself as he left Mr. Taylor's class headed to the bus. He started his bus and prepared to make the drop off trip for his passengers and then make his way home.

CHAPTER 2

RONALD THE SCHOOL BUS DRIVER

Ronald would leave our home from the back door entrance and down a few steps onto the ground. He would walk over to the bus that was park in our huge backyard. He open the door and sat in the drivers seat. During the winter cold months he would start the school bus and let it run for about 30 minutes before he would move the bus. The other months he would start and wait about 10 minutes before he drove the school bus up the steep bank, turn right onto Barhamville road. We could hear the roaring sounds of the bus as he picked up speed while we walked to school. Ronald drove his bus about thirty minutes before picking up his students at the various stops. "Good morning! How are you doing?", he asked as the students entered the bus. "Hey Ronald", responded the students as they got on the bus with many books wrapped in their arms. Regardless if the weather was sunny, hot, cold, or rainy, Ronald's students waited for their bus driver and to sit on their brownish leather seats. Now and then, Ronald would look in the mirror above his head to glimpse at his sleepy passengers while driving up and down the dirt roads, making his way back to school everyday. Approaching the bus drop off area on the school ground, you could hear Ronald's warning, "Watch your steps", as the students left the bus. After parking the bus in the parking area, Ronald went to check his locker and checked in at his homeroom.

After the first period bell Ronald was off to the first period classes for the day, which was Calculus. He felt so thrilled every time he went to class because of his passion for the subject matter.

CHAPTER 3
CAREER DAY

Teaching Calculus and Trigonometry was fun and exciting for the students who came to his classes. At the end of the day, Ronald returned to his bus and the students begin to load up his bus. "See you tomorrow", said Ronald after each stop. He drove himself back home. He parked his bus in the backyard and went inside.

CHAPTER 4
GOOD DEEDS GET WISDOM

Mom heard a knock at the door. After Mark and mom greeted each other, Mark begin to walk toward Ronald's room. Mark had so many questions to ask Ronald. "What are we doing for the Easter Holidays? "Nothing much other than going to the big Easter Program at Bethel A.M.E. church and the Easter Egg Hunt at Allen University. "You want to go?", asked Ronald. We might as well as they both looked at each other and laughed.

"What awards are you getting this year?', Mark asked his cousin as the two seniors were walking towards the front porch.

"I'll probably get an award in math," Ronald said. After much conservation while standing on the front porch. Mark turned toward Ronald before he got into his car and said, "You know that I am going to A & T College to become an Electrical Engineer".

"Man, I am applying for the same college and in the same field too", said Ronald. Let's talk some more after graduation. See you at school next week. Mark drove off and Ronald went inside our home.

The Awards Day was a few days before graduation. Our parents always supported us by attending school functions all during the year. Since, we lived so close to the school, our parents left home early enough to walk to school and get the best seat in the auditorium. They chose the middle isle and near the front. Mom had on a beautiful sky blue dress, held a blue purse, and had shoes to match. Dad had on his navy blue suit and black shoes.

The proud moment came when Dr. Johnson, the principle commanded. "Will the bus drivers come up to the platform?" As the drivers came forward, Dr. Johnson gave each one a driving certificate. "Take a look at the first bus drivers at C.A. Johnson High School". Each driver shook our principle hand and received a check for $25.00 for having a safe driving record, hard work and clean buses. The entire audience clapped and gave the drivers a standing ovation.

CHAPTER 5
THE BIG DECISION

Just a week before graduation and all the seniors were getting antsy around the school. No more tests, no more getting up and driving the school bus and hanging around with my classmatas, while talking to his younger brother and looking through the year book together in their living room. Ronald had this big calendar in his room and at the end of each day, he would cross out that day on the calendar. "We are down to two days before Graduation Day," said Ronald to his family.

The next day Ronald had gone to Daves' Barber Shop where his dad had cut his hair. Mom brought his suit home from the Moore Clearners and his younger brother had polished and shine his black shoes.

Graduation day was held at the Town Ship Auditorium on Taylor Street. Everyone sat quietly, the drummers began to play, and the graduation march begain. One of the proudest moments in our parents life was to see their first born son to graduate from high school. More than a hundred students graduated in the class of 1959.

After the graduates marched out to the front of the auditorium, family members and friends met to take pictures. Group pictures were taken, and family pictures were taken. While mom and dad were standing taking pictures and congratulating some of our neighborhood seniors, they overheard a classmates asked Ronald what his plans were for the future. "I plan to attend North Carolina A & T College", Ronald said to his classmate. Our parents were very happy when they heard of their son big decision.

Mom had prepared a small reception at our home for their son, friends, and their family. Our mom made a delicious potato salad with fried chicken. About nine o'clock mom and I began to clean up.

CHAPTER 6
WORDS OF WISDOM

June and July were two months of preparing Ronald to go to college. Dad took care of the oil, oil filler and tires. Mom went shopping when ever she saw bedspreads, sheets, facetowels, and bath towels on sale, while I would wash clothes and hang the clothes on the clothes line in our backyard to dry. I would iron shirts, neatly fold his sweaters and then place them in the footlockers along with other items.

Ronald took three of the footlockers to the Greyhound Bus Station and mailed the lockers off to his new address.

The night before we left, dad and Ronald packed the truck with the luggage and a few bags. About three A.M. the next morning we began to pack our lunches and sodas in the back seat where mom and I sat. Dad was driving and Ronald sat in the passenger's seat. Driving along the old Number One Highway that was very, very dark would put us to sleep right away. There were no super highways, just a two lane highway with no street lights and no GPS for specific directions. Dad had a map and a flash light that Ronald would hold to locate the next town and the big cities. We slept for many miles to North Carolina. After one of the many stops for gas, mom began her words of wisdom talking to her son. "We know you are going to do very well in all of your subjects. Remember what we taught you Ronald, about our family values such as, "be kind to others, be honest, and do unto others as you would have them do to you". The first year away from home may be a little hard but you will adjust and do great things. "Stand up for what you believe is right for your family, community, and yourself, regardless of what people may think of you. Saluted with the words of wisdom from mom, Ronald eventually took another nap, while thinking about her words.

Ron woke up, he saw his mom and dad stretching their legs and arms in front of the dorm. They told him this is his new home for a year. At the front entrance we were greeted by the director who showed us his room. Dad and Ron went to the office to take care of business while mom and I began to decorate his bare room.

Ronald T. Martin   James Paterson   Mark Martin

CHAPTER 7

SIT–INS

Ronald, his cousin Mark Marin and their best friend, James Patterson were the 3 students from A & T College who sat down on the lunch counters stools at Woolworth Store on February 2, 1960. As these sit-ins spread throughout the South, did not bring fear to the young college students. They were willing to STAND UP! for their rights to end segregation, No more whites on one side and the other side for colored people to sit at the counter. At the age of 19, all three students had to sit all day to be spit on, call names, and being harassed by the people behind the counter as well as others who came into the restaurant. Scared, terrified of the unknown what could happen to them, sat patiently at the counter and who wanted to be serve some coffee.

CHAPTER 8

THE SIT-IN MOVEMENT
MY BROTHER'S PART

After registration and paying the bills, classes began. By the month of October, Ronald started his routine of going to classes and then to the library everyday.

There was a phone booth at the end of the hallway not too far from his room. Every other week he would call collect and tell us stories about what was going on in and out of the class. One call came through and he told mom that he was going to participate in the Sit-in Movements that started at A & T College. They were told to sit at the lunch counter at the segragated F.L. Woolworth Store and ask for a cup of coffee.

James Patterson, Ronald and Mark Martin all from South Carolina, were the three students from A & T College who sat down at the lunch counter stools on February 2,

1960. They were willing to STAND UP! for what they believe was the right thing to do, to end segragated lunch counters by refusing to leave a whites only lunch counter at which they were denied service.

OVERVIEW

My book, STAND UP! For What You Believe in is about my oldest brother and his legacy in The Sit-In Movement in Greensboro, North Carolina at the segregated Woolworth Lunchcounter. Ronald, our cousin Mark Martin and their best friend James Patterson, who helped make a difference in all of our lives.

They helped inspire all students and parents to speak out, to stand up for what is right, and to give hope to all people who are reluctant to speak out. Sometimes in life, we go along with the crowd, whether the crowd is right or wrong. I believe life is not like that at all.

I believe an individual has a choice to stand up for what they believe in and be accountable regardless of who stands with you or not. If you are a student under the age of 18 years old, you might want to discuss the issue with your parents what you want to do and why you want to stand up for your beliefs.

In a more spiritual realm in life, I remember Jesus called his disciples and said to them, "If anyone intends to come after Me, Let him deny (forget, ignore, disown, and lose sight of himself and his own interest) and take up the cross, and (joining Me as a disciple and siding with My party) follow with Me (continually, cleaving steadfastly to Me)". (Amplified Bible—Mark 8:34).

EXPLANATION OF PICTURES

Our first family home in Pinehurst.

Our mom and dad
Bruce and Ronald

Ronald and Bruce
sitting on a big chair.

Warren Benjamin Martin
Our youngest brother

Ronald Martin, James Patterson
at Woolworth Lunch Counter.

THE CIVIL RIGHTS MOVEMENT

Our dad receiving an outstanding driver's award
from the U.S. Postal Service.

Family tree taken
my brother Bruce Martin.

Printed in the United States
By Bookmasters